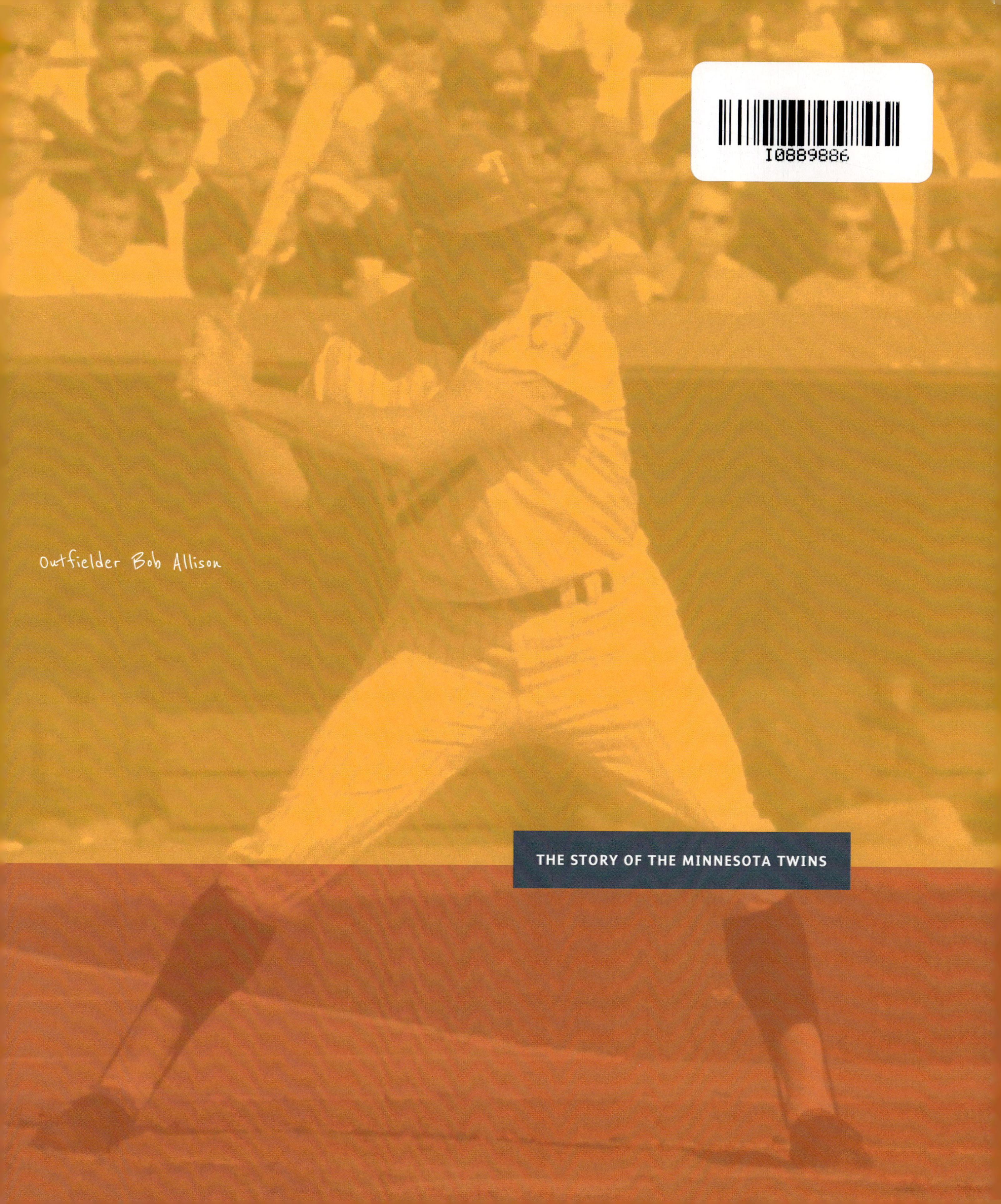
Outfielder Bob Allison

THE STORY OF THE MINNESOTA TWINS

Pitcher Pablo López

THE STORY OF THE

MINNESOTA TWINS

JOE TISCHLER

CREATIVE SPORTS

Pitcher Johan Santana

CREATIVE EDUCATION / CREATIVE PAPERBACKS

Published by Creative Education and Creative Paperbacks
P.O. Box 227, Mankato, Minnesota 56002
Creative Education and Creative Paperbacks are imprints of
The Creative Company
www.thecreativecompany.us

Book Design by Wyeth/Graham Morgan
Art direction by Blue Design (www.bluedes.com)

Images by Alamy Stock Photo/Tim Warner, 28–29; Getty Images/Anthony Neste, 10, B Bennett, 7 (bottom, left), Bettmann, 1, Bill Polo, 9, Brace Hemmelgarn, 6 (bottom, right), Bruce Kluckhohn, 20, Carlos Gonzalez/Star Tribune, 30, David Durochik/Diamond, cover, Diamond Images, cover, 6 (top, left), Focus On Sport, 6 (bottom, left), 18, George Kubas/Diamond Images, 31, Gregory Shamus, 23, Hank Walker/Time Life Pictures, 16, John Williamson, 3, Jon SooHoo, 19, Kelly Gavin, 2, Louis Requena, 7 (top, right), National Baseball Hall of Fame Library, 7 (bottom, right), Otto Greule Jr, 6 (top, right), Richard Mackson, 11, Rob Leiter, 4–5, 32, Stephen Dunn, 10, TIM CLARY, 7 (top, left), Tim Umphrey, 27, Underwood Archives, 12; Wikimedia Commons/Bain News Service, publisher, 15, Tim Wilson, 24–25

Library of Congress Cataloging-in-Publication Data
Names: Tischler, Joe author
Title: The story of the Minnesota Twins / by Joe Tischler.
Description: Mankato, Minnesota : Creative Education and Creative Paperbacks, [2026] | Series: Creative sports. Major League baseball | Includes index. | Audience: Ages 8-12 | Audience: Grades 4-6 | Summary: "Discover the Minnesota Twins' thrilling journey from their origins in Washington to World Series wins and recent seasons, featuring legendary players, dramatic victories, and the Major League Baseball team's enduring fan support. Written for middle-grade readers. Includes table of contents, sidebars, and index"– Provided by publisher.
Identifiers: LCCN 2025021255 (print) | LCCN 2025021256 (ebook) | ISBN 9798895811009 library binding | ISBN 9798896800538 paperback | ISBN 9798895812266 ebook
Subjects: LCSH: Minnesota Twins (Baseball team)–History–Juvenile literature | Baseball–Minnesota–History, Local–Juvenile literature | LCGFT: Literature.
Classification: LCC GV875.M55 T583 2026 (print) | LCC GV875.M55 (ebook) | DDC 796.357/6409776579–dc23/eng/20250626
LC record available at https://lccn.loc.gov/2025021255
LC ebook record available at https://lccn.loc.gov/2025021256

Printed in the United States

First baseman Justin Morneau

Twins

Twins

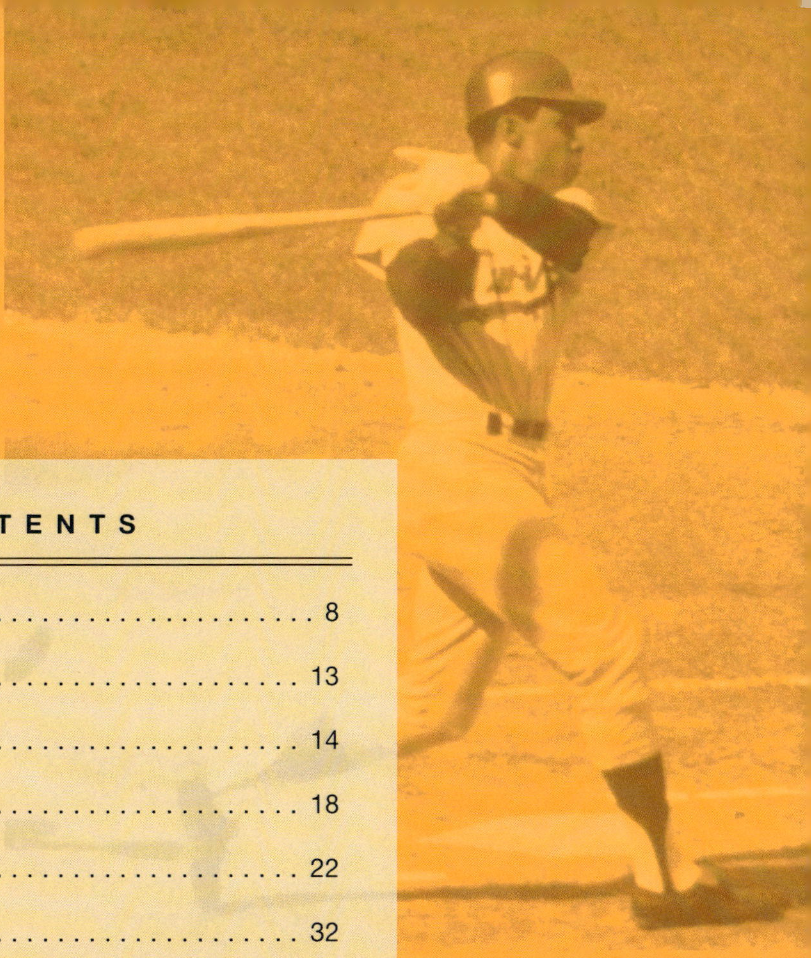

CONTENTS

EXTRA INNINGS

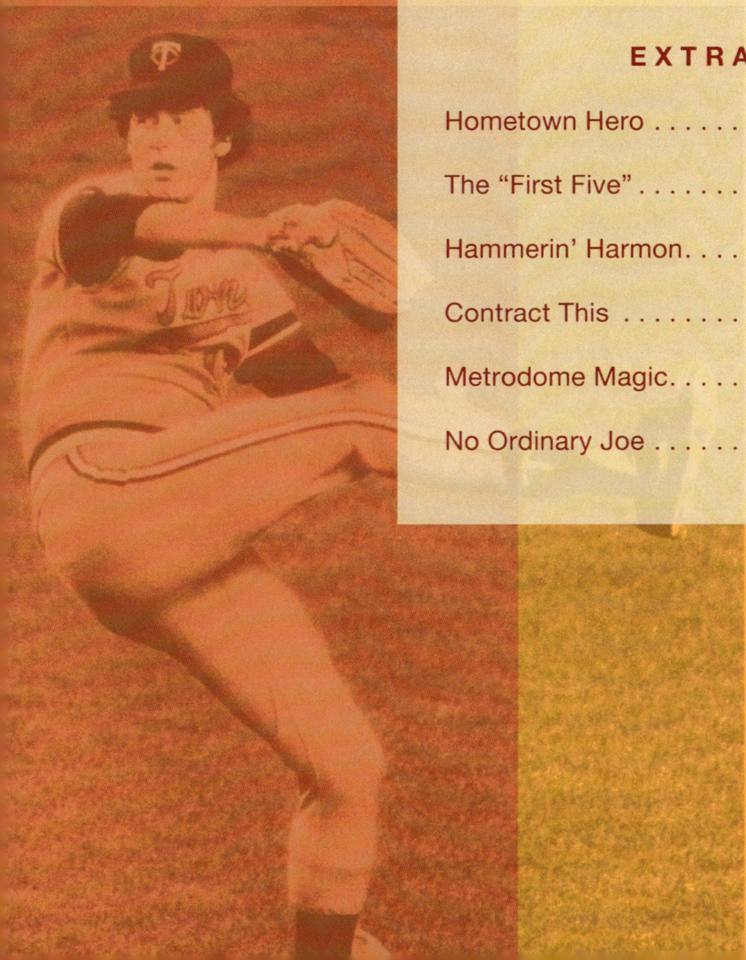

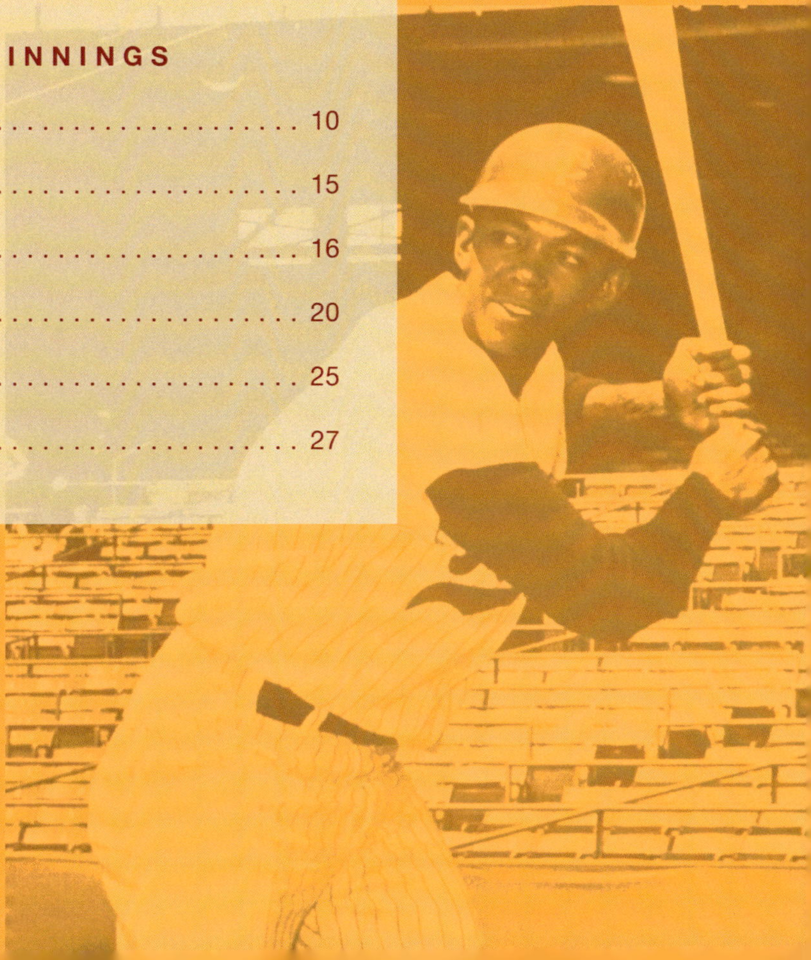

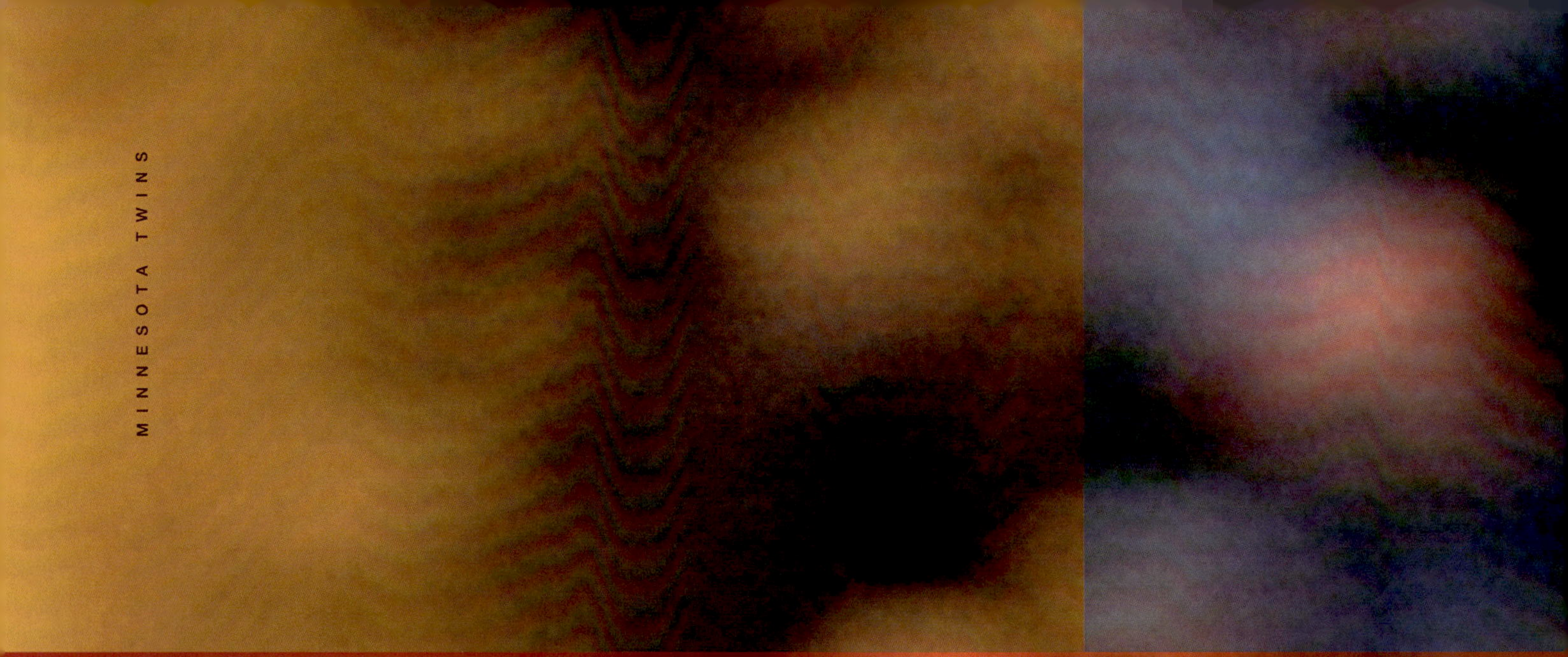

PUCKETT POWER

The 1991 World Series was known as the "Worst to First" World Series. Both the Atlanta Braves and Minnesota Twins were last in their respective divisions the previous season. Four of the first five games of the series were tight contests. The game-winning run was scored during the final play in two of the games. The Braves won those games. They held a 3–2 series lead. Game 6 was played at the Twins home stadium, Hubert H. Humphrey Metrodome.

The Twins needed to win to stay alive. All-Star center fielder Kirby Puckett did all he could to keep their world championship dreams going. In the bottom of the first inning, he drilled a run-producing triple down the left field line. He later scored on a Shane Mack single to left field. The Twins led 2–0.

Puckett used his glove to keep the Braves off the scoreboard in the top of the third inning. Braves center fielder Ron Gant launched a deep shot to left-center field. Puckett sprinted to the ball, jumped high against the plexiglass outfield wall, and snatched the base hit away from Gant. Minnesota still led 2–0.

Center fielder Kirby Puckett

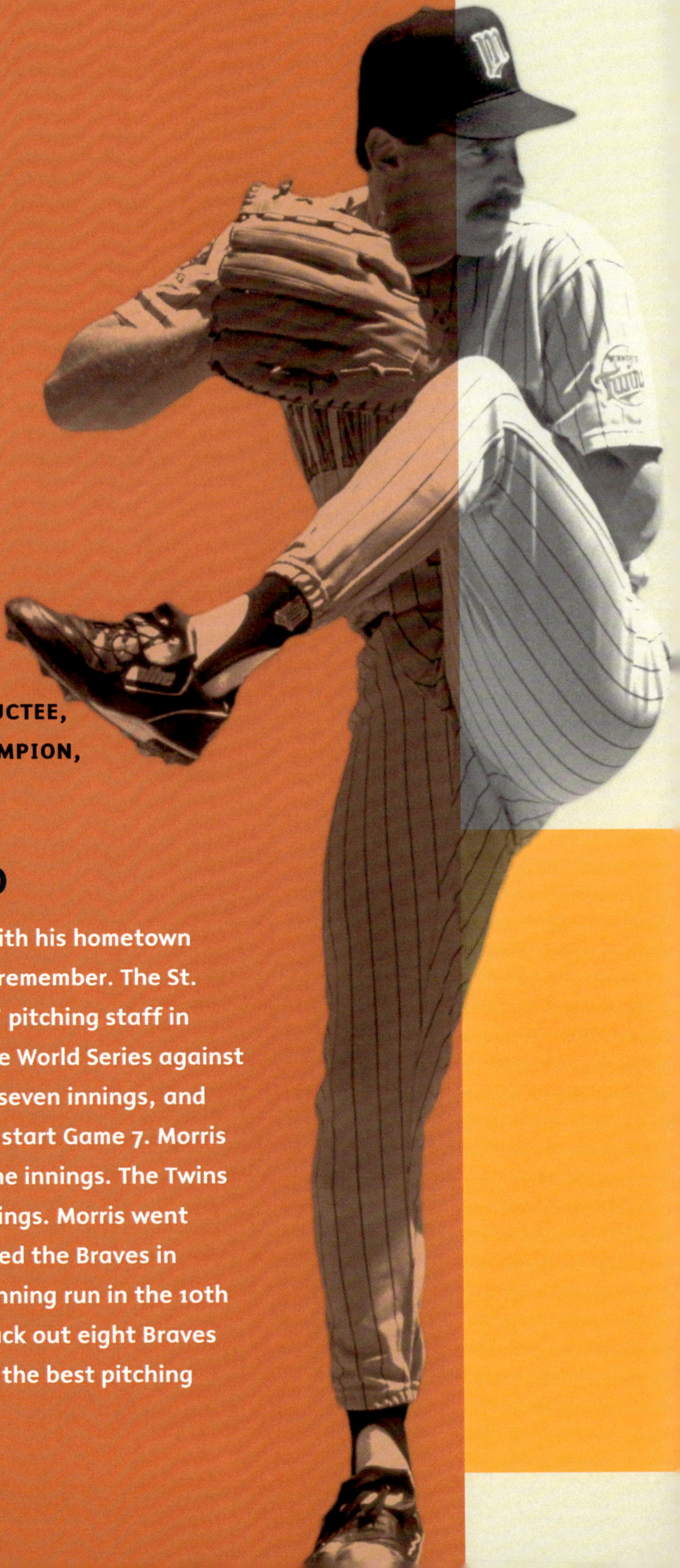

JACK MORRIS
PITCHER
TWINS SEASONS: 1991
HEIGHT: 6-FOOT-3
WEIGHT: 195 POUNDS
KEY STATS: 2018 HALL OF FAME INDUCTEE, 5X ALL-STAR, 4X WORLD SERIES CHAMPION, 1991 WORLD SERIES MVP

HOMETOWN HERO

Jack Morris played only one season with his hometown Minnesota Twins. It was a season to remember. The St. Paul native was the ace of the Twins' pitching staff in 1991. He was the Game 1 starter in the World Series against Atlanta. He allowed only two runs in seven innings, and the Twins won 5–2. He got the call to start Game 7. Morris held the Braves scoreless through nine innings. The Twins did not score either through nine innings. Morris went back out for the 10th inning. He retired the Braves in order. The Twins scored the game-winning run in the 10th on a hit from Gene Larkin. Morris struck out eight Braves batters. His game is regarded as one the best pitching performances in World Series history.

Outfielder Dan Gladden

Atlanta tied the game in the fifth inning on a two-run home run from Terry Pendleton. Puckett's bat helped Minnesota regain the lead in the bottom half of the inning. His sacrifice fly scored Dan Gladden to give Minnesota a 3–2 lead. Atlanta scored a run in the seventh to tie the game 3–3.

Neither team scored in the eighth or ninth innings. The game went to extra innings. Twins closer Rick Aguilera held Atlanta scoreless in the 10th and 11th innings. Puckett led off the bottom of the 11th inning against new Braves pitcher Charlie Leibrandt. Puckett told on-deck batter Chili Davis he planned to bunt for a base hit. Davis responded by saying, "Bunt? No. Hit it out and let's go home." On the fourth pitch of the at-bat, Puckett lifted a deep shot over the left-center field wall for a game-winning home run. CBS announcer Jack Buck said on-air as the ball went over the fence, "And we'll see you tomorrow night." The Twins won the next night to take the series.

Puckett's home run is immortalized in Twins history. The Metrodome had blue seats. The seat where the home run ball landed was changed to gold. It remained there until the Metrodome was torn down in 2014. At Target Field, a statue of Puckett pumping his fists while rounding the bases after his home run stands outside Gate 34 at the Twins' new home.

"THE BIG TRAIN"

The Twins' history began far from Minnesota in 1901. The American League (AL) was founded that year. One of the teams was the Washington Senators. They were based in Washington, D.C. They weren't very good. They suffered through 11 straight losing seasons. The worst was 1904. They won just 38 games. The team was so bad that famed sportswriter Charles Dryden wrote, "Washington: First in war, first in peace, and last in the American League." That phrase was a takeoff on a speech in honor of George Washington after he died. He was "First in war, first in peace, and first in the hearts of his countrymen."

The team's first big star was pitcher Walter Johnson. He joined the Senators in 1907. The 19-year-old won just five games in his first season. By 1912, he improved to 33 wins. The Senators compiled a 91–61 mark that year. It was their first winning season. Johnson won a Major League Baseball (MLB) best 36 games in 1913. That earned him the league's Most Valuable Player (MVP) award.

For several years, most of the players around Johnson were not especially good. The Senators finally won the AL pennant in 1924. Nicknamed "The Big Train" for the speed of his fastballs, Johnson was again named MVP. Left fielder Goose Goslin led the offense. He hit .344. He smacked 12 home runs and drove in 129 runs. Right fielder Sam Rice chipped in with a .334 batting average.

Washington faced the New York Giants in the 1924 World Series. The teams traded wins in the first six games. In Game 7, Washington trailed 3–1 in the bottom of the eighth inning. There were two outs. The bases were loaded. Second baseman Bucky Harris hit a ground ball to third base. It hopped and bounced

Pitcher Walter Johnson

away. Two runners scored to tie the game. In the bottom of the 12th, outfielder Earl McNeely hit an almost identical bad-hop ball. It drove in the winning run.

The Senators returned to the World Series the next season. They faced the Pittsburgh Pirates. Washington held a 3–1 series lead. But the Pirates won the final three games to take the title. Johnson retired after the 1927 season. He had 417 career wins, second in MLB history only to Cy Young's 511.

The Senators continued to perform well without Johnson. Washington won a franchise-best 99 games in 1933. It returned to the World Series. But it lost to the New York Giants in five games. After several losing seasons, they came close to another World Series in 1945. They finished just behind the Detroit Tigers in the AL. During the next 15 years, they had just one winning season. Attendance suffered. Team owner Calvin Griffith wanted to give the team a fresh start.

MOVING TO MINNESOTA

In November 1960, Griffith announced that the franchise would move to the Minneapolis-St. Paul area in Minnesota. The two cities were nicknamed the "Twin Cities." So Griffith changed the team's name to the Minnesota Twins.

Following the move, the team played home games in Metropolitan Stadium. It finished 70–90 in its first Minnesota season. The Twins won 91 games in each of the next two seasons. Powerful infielder and left fielder Harmon Killebrew became a star. So did shortstop Zoilo Versalles. Right fielder Tony Oliva was named AL Rookie of the Year in 1964. On the mound, Minnesota featured lefty pitcher Jim Kaat.

In 1965, the Twins won a franchise-record 102 games. They won their first AL pennant in Minnesota. Versalles led the league in seven categories.

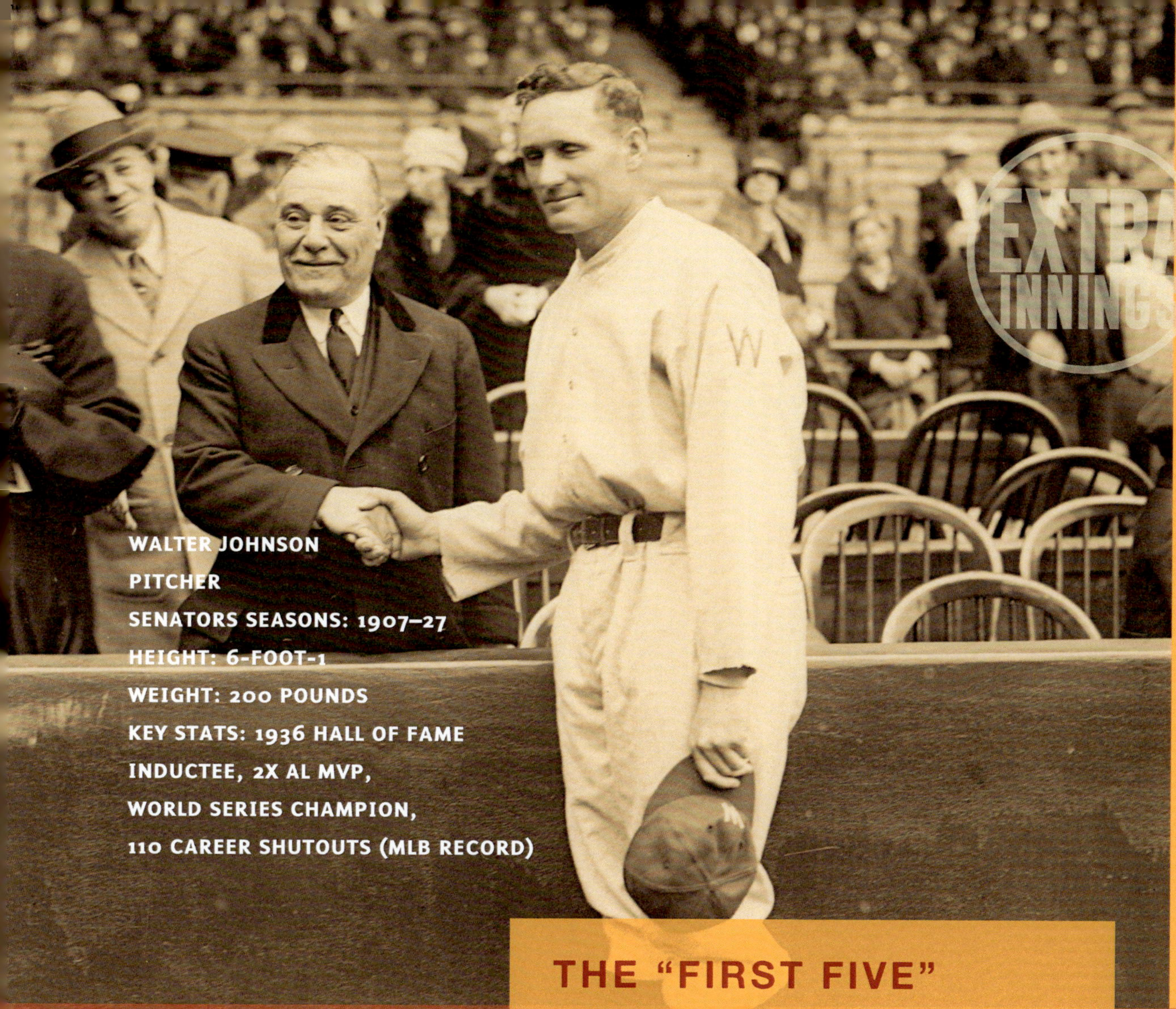

EXTRA INNINGS

WALTER JOHNSON
PITCHER
SENATORS SEASONS: 1907–27
HEIGHT: 6-FOOT-1
WEIGHT: 200 POUNDS
KEY STATS: 1936 HALL OF FAME INDUCTEE, 2X AL MVP, WORLD SERIES CHAMPION, 110 CAREER SHUTOUTS (MLB RECORD)

THE "FIRST FIVE"

The Baseball Hall of Fame in Cooperstown, New York, began inducting members in 1936. There were five members of the first class. They were position players Ty Cobb, Babe Ruth, and Honus Wagner and pitchers Christy Mathewson and Walter Johnson. It was easy to see why Johnson was among the "First Five." Johnson pitched 21 seasons. He led the AL in strikeouts 12 times. Six times he led the league in wins, including 36 in 1913. He won AL MVP that year and again in 1924. That year, he helped the franchise win its first World Series. His MLB record of 110 career shutouts is widely considered unbreakable.

EXTRA INNINGS

HARMON KILLEBREW
THIRD BASEMAN/FIRST BASEMAN/ LEFT FIELDER
SENATORS/TWINS SEASONS: 1954–74
HEIGHT: 6-FOOT-0
WEIGHT: 195 POUNDS
KEY STATS: 1984 HALL OF FAME INDUCTEE, 13X ALL-STAR, 1969 AL MVP, 573 CAREER HOME RUNS

HAMMERIN' HARMON

Harmon Killebrew broke into the Washington Senators' lineup in 1954. At 18 years old, he was the youngest player in the major leagues. It was just the start of his long career as a power hitter. He soon became known as "Killer." Killebrew's breakout season came in 1959. He belted 42 home runs. In 1967, he slugged the longest home run in Twins history. The ball soared nearly 520 feet. It landed in the sixth row of the upper deck of Metropolitan Stadium. The Mall of America now sits on the land where the stadium once stood. Inside the mall, a plaque marks where home plate once was and 520 feet from there is a red-painted seat which marks the location of where Killebrew's home run ball landed. He finished his career with 573 home runs.

He was named AL MVP. The Twins faced the Los Angeles Dodgers in the World Series. The teams split the first six games. In Game 7, Dodgers ace pitcher Sandy Koufax shut out the Twins 2–0.

The Twins bolstered their lineup in 1967. They added second baseman Rod Carew. His superb batting helped him win the AL Rookie of the Year award. Years later, teammate Steve Brye noted, "Rod Carew could get more hits with a soup bone than I could get with a rack full of bats." The Twins went 91–71 that season. But the Boston Red Sox slipped ahead of them to take the pennant by a single game.

Two years later, the AL and National League (NL) each split into two divisions. Minnesota landed in the AL West Division. The Twins won the division that season and the following year. The Baltimore Orioles swept them in the AL Championship Series (ALCS) both times.

The Twins hovered near the .500 mark throughout the 1970s. Griffith replaced the majority of the team's veterans with younger, less expensive players. In 1981, the Twins celebrated 20 years of big-league baseball in Minnesota. But they finished last in the AL West. Attendance at Metropolitan Stadium gradually dropped.

In 1982, the team moved into the Hubert H. Humphrey Metrodome. It stood in downtown Minneapolis. The Metrodome was an indoor stadium. Its roof looked like a big bubble. Unfortunately, the team's 60–102 mark was its worst since moving to Minnesota.

At the same time, however, new standouts were bubbling up. Rookie first baseman Kent Hrbek batted .301 that season. He was named an All-Star. Hard-hitting Gary Gaetti played third base. He had high energy and a sure glove. Right fielder Tom Brunansky wielded a booming bat.

Right fielder Tom Brunansky

Minnesota picked up center fielder Kirby Puckett in the 1982 MLB Draft. He broke into the Twins' starting lineup in 1984. His nonstop hustle and ever-present smile quickly endeared himself to fans. That same year, crafty left-hander Frank Viola began to lead the pitching staff.

TWIN TITLES

Late in the 1986 season, Minnesota made a pivotal move. It hired 36-year-old Tom Kelly to manage the team. Under his guidance, the Twins quickly improved. "We just do what T. K. [Kelly] tells us," Puckett explained. "Just go out, give 100 percent, and we'll win the battle one game at a time."

That approach paid off. Hrbek, Puckett, Gaetti, and Brunansky all slugged at least 28 home runs in 1987. The upstart Twins won the AL West

First baseman Kent Hrbek

Joe Mauer bats at Target Field.

EXTRA INNINGS

CONTRACT THIS

Following the 2001 season, a majority of MLB team owners voted to eliminate two teams for the 2002 season. The teams expected to be contracted were the Twins and the Montreal Expos. There were economic reasons for the contraction plan. The Twins and Expos did not make enough money, and the teams did not have plans to build new ballparks to replace their outdated ones. Thankfully for players and fans of the teams, the plan fell through. A Minnesota court ruled the Twins had to honor their lease with the Metrodome. The Twins eventually built their new ballpark, Target Field, which opened in 2010. The Expos relocated to Washington, D.C. in 2005 and were renamed the Washington Nationals.

Division. They upset the Detroit Tigers in the ALCS in five games. For the first time in 22 years, the Twins were in the World Series. The Twins held home-field advantage in the World Series. That was a big edge to Minnesota. It led MLB with 56 home wins in 1987. The raucous fans waving their white "Homer Hankies" gave the Twins another edge. The teams split the first six games of the series. The home team won each game. Game 7 was in Minnesota. Twins ace Viola pitched eight strong innings. He lived up to his nickname of "Sweet Music." The Twins won 4–2. They claimed their first championship in Minnesota.

By 1990, the team stumbled back into last place. They struggled out of the gates in 1991. Minnesota lost 9 of their first 11 games. The Twins started to improve. But by the end of May, they were still two games under .500 and 5.5 games out of first place. Minnesota went on a heater to start June. It won the first 15 games of the month. The Twins now led the division. It was a lead they would hold the rest of the season. A key reason for the improvement was second-year pitcher Scott Erickson. After losing his first two starts of the season, Erickson rattled off 12 straight wins. That streak included four complete-game efforts with three shut outs. He was in line to start for the AL in the All-Star Game. But he was injured. Teammate Jack Morris started in his place.

The Twins trounced the Toronto Blue Jays in the ALCS in five games. They met the Atlanta Braves. Minnesota, again, held home-field advantage. The teams battled through seven nail-biting games. Five games were decided by a single run. Puckett's brilliance in Game 6 forced a Game 7. The matchup was scoreless through nine innings. Morris had pitched the first nine innings. Kelly told Morris he would send in a reliever. But Morris was determined on staying in the game. "I would have needed a shotgun to get him out of the game," said Kelly. "And I didn't have one." Morris pitched a perfect 10th. The Twins scored the winning run in the bottom of the inning. The Twins were champions for the second time in five seasons. Like in 1987, the home team won every game of the series.

Minnesota had a winning record the following season. But it missed the playoffs. The 1993 season started a string of eight straight losing seasons. Puckett developed blurred vision before the 1996 season. It forced him to retire.

The 2001 season was a season of opportunity for the Twins. The young nucleus included outfielders Torii Hunter and Jacque Jones and infielders Doug Mientkiewicz and Cristian Guzmán. The pitching staff was led by All-Stars Brad Radke, Joe Milton, and Joe Mays. The team raced out to a 34–17 record through May. It held a five-game lead in the AL Central through mid-July. But the Twins began to fade. Minnesota finished 85–77. But the Cleveland Indians caught them for the division title.

POSTSEASON PROBLEMS

Minnesota turned the promise of the 2001 season into a division title in 2002. It returned to the playoffs for the first time in 11 years. The team pulled out a thrilling win over the Oakland Athletics in the AL Division Series (ALDS). It faced the Anaheim Angels in the ALCS. But the Angels won in five games.

Minnesota repeated as division champs in 2003 and 2004. But the New York Yankees knocked them out of the playoffs both seasons. Two new stars

Pitcher Brad Radke

Wilson
Twins
22

WCCO
NEWS•TALK
830
Budweiser
Boston Scientific
408ft.

EXTRA INNINGS

METRODOME MAGIC

The Hubert H. Humphrey Metrodome was full of quirks. Among them was the dome's light-colored roof. Opposing players complained of losing track of fly balls. In the 1987 and 1991 World Series, the Twins held home-field advantage. The 1987 series win over St. Louis was the first World Series where the home team won each game. The same thing happened in the 1991 World Series. The final season at the Metrodome was 2009. The regular season was extended by one game for a tiebreaker game. The Twins defeated Detroit in extra innings to win the AL Central.

emerged: starting pitcher Johan Santana and closer Joe Nathan. In 2004, Santana won the AL Cy Young Award and Nathan had 44 saves.

The Twins missed the playoffs in 2005. The following season was full of individual and team achievements. Catcher Joe Mauer won the first of his three batting titles with a .347 average. First baseman Justin Morneau was named AL MVP. He batted .321 with 34 home runs and 130 runs batted in (RBI). Santana won his second AL Cy Young Award in three seasons. The Twins won 96 games. They overtook Detroit on the final day of the season to win the division. But Oakland swept them in the ALDS.

Mauer won his second batting title in 2008. The Twins tied the Chicago White Sox for the division lead. A one-game tiebreaker was needed to determine the division champion. The Twins lost the game on the road, 1–0. The following year was similar. The Twins tied the Tigers for the division lead. Another tiebreaker game was needed. This time, the Twins won a thrilling game, 6–5, in 12 innings. But the Yankees swept the Twins in the playoffs.

The Twins opened their new ballpark, Target Field, in 2010. It was an outdoor stadium. The Twins did well in their new home. They won the division again. But they were swept by the Yankees, again, in the playoffs.

Rocco Baldelli became manager in 2019. It was a record-setting season. The team won 101 games and the division. The "Bomba Squad" belted an MLB record of 307 home runs. Five players hit more than 30 home runs. Designated hitter Nelson Cruz led the squad with 41 home runs. The power did not help in the playoffs. The Yankees swept them in the ALDS.

The Twins were division champions again in the COVID-shortened 2020 season. They went 36–24. Minnesota hosted the Houston Astros in the AL Wild

EXTRA INNINGS

NO ORDINARY JOE

Joe Mauer was not just a great baseball player. He was a great athlete. In his senior year of high school, the St. Paul native became the only athlete ever to be named National Player of the Year in two sports (football and baseball). He earned a scholarship to play quarterback at Florida State University. But his love was baseball. A natural hitter, Mauer struck out only once in his four-year high school career. His hometown Twins selected him with the first overall pick in the 2001 MLB Draft. In 2006, Mauer became the first catcher in AL history to win the batting title. He did it two more times in 2008 and 2009. Mauer's best year came in 2009. He batted .365 and was named AL MVP.

JOE MAUER
CATCHER/FIRST BASEMAN
TWINS SEASONS: 2004–18
HEIGHT: 6-FOOT-5
WEIGHT: 225 POUNDS
KEY STATS: 2024 HALL OF FAME INDUCTEE, 3X BATTING CHAMPION, 6X ALL-STAR, 2009 AL MVP

R Chirinos

Center fielder hitter Byron Buxton

4

Catcher Ryan Jeffers

Card Series (ALWCS). Houston swept the best-of-three series. The Twins had now lost 18 straight postseason games dating back to 2004. That set a record for the longest postseason losing streak across the four male professional leagues in North America (MLB, National Football League, National Basketball Association, and National Hockey League).

Minnesota returned to the playoffs in 2023. It was guided by starting pitchers Pablo López, Sonny Gray, and Joe Ryan. The team would finally end their postseason losing streak with a 3–1 victory over Toronto in the first game of the ALWCS. The Twins also won the next game and advanced to the ALDS. There, they fell to Houston. The Twins faltered down the stretch in 2024 and missed the playoffs.

The Minnesota Twins' history spans more than a century. It includes relocation, world championships, and legendary players. If the Twins can realize their full potential, Minnesota may soon be decorating Target Field with more championship banners.

Shortstop Carlos Correa

INDEX